LIKE WOW! The Mystery of Light!

by Ailynn Collins

I0820873

CAPSTONE PRESS
a capstone imprint

Published by Capstone Press, an imprint of Capstone
1710 Roe Crest Drive, North Mankato, Minnesota 56003
capstonepub.com

Library of Congress Cataloging-in-Publication Data
is available on the Library of Congress website.

ISBN: 9798875214165 (hardcover)
ISBN: 9798875214332 (paperback)
ISBN: 9798875214349 (ebook PDF)

Summary: The world gets a little brighter as Scooby and the Mystery Inc. gang illuminate the science of light. From light's sources and speed to rainbows and eyesight, uncover light's brilliant secrets.

Editorial Credits
Editor: Christopher Harbo; Designer: Tracy Davies; Media Researcher: Svetlana Zhurkin; Production Specialist: Whitney Schaefer

Image Credits
Getty Images: Ali Majdfar, 10, mariya_rosemary, 25 (bottom); Shutterstock: al7, 22, AlinaMD, 8, Anton Starikov, 13 (bowl), Cartooncux (beaker), cover and throughout, Creative Travel Projects, 29, Designua, cover and throughout (light bulb), 28, Elena Zajchikova, 7 (flowerpot), Everett Collection, 23 (back), Fahd Almadany, 5, Florian Nimsdorf, 9, grayjay, 19, Ground Picture, 21, hideto999, 17, HobbitArt (science icons), cover and throughout, imageBROKER, 24, Maria Martyshova (background), cover and throughout, Michael C. Gray, 13 (pitcher), Mike Workman, 13 (back), Montypeter, 14, mr_bom, 11 (back), muratart, 12, NataliaZa, 11 (sparkler), Oksana Ermak, 25 (top), Olga Popova, 18 (water glass), Paul Aniszewski, 7 (back), petrroudny43, 23 (prism), Photo B Studio, 13 (lemons), Pixel-Shot, 16, Raland, 4, Sky Blue Photography, 6, Toxa2x2, 26, Uuganbayar, 18 (back), WaffelBoo, 15, Yuliia Sonsedska, 11 (raccoon), zombiu26, 20, Zonda, 27

Printed and bound in China. PO 006276

Table of Contents

What Is Light?

Summer is almost over. While the days are still warm, the Mystery Inc. gang is excited to spend a long weekend in nature. They found a cool spot in a forest by a lake and have set up their campsite.

This place is in-*tents*-ly cool, Scoob!

I love *ruffing* it!

Like, wow! What a fun evening! The sun has just set and it is getting dark. Fred has built a cozy campfire. Shaggy and Scooby chase glowing fireflies.

Uh-oh! Velma is in trouble. She has dropped her glasses. Luckily, Daphne has her flashlight handy.

Do you see what each member of the gang has in common? Did you guess that they're all using light? You're right! But have you thought about what light really is?

Light is a form of energy. In science, energy is defined as the ability to do work. Sound, heat, and electricity are also forms of energy. But light is the only form of energy that we can see with our eyes. And the special name for light energy is electromagnetic radiation.

Light is important to all living things. People and animals need light to see the world around us. We also need light and darkness to know when to sleep or wake up. Light even helps animals know when to look for food or hunt.

And don't forget about plants! They need light to grow and make food. The amount of sunlight flowers get also tells them when to bloom.

FACT

Sunlight can be harnessed as solar energy and stored in batteries. It's an unlimited and clean form of power.

Sources of Light

Hey, gang, have you ever thought about where light comes from? Scientists classify the sources of light as either natural or artificial. Natural sources are any types of light that exist without the help of humans. Artificial sources are those made by people.

The most important natural source of light is the sun. The sun is our nearest star, giving us light and heat. Millions and millions of stars in the universe also give off light and heat.

Sun-sational light!

Jinkies! Light can come from Earth's darkest depths!

Lightning gives off light, as do fires. When fires start naturally, like after a lightning strike, we count them as natural sources of light. When volcanoes erupt, they spew molten lava that gives off light as well.

FACT

Small particles from the sun clash with the gases in our planet's atmosphere. The energy they release creates the colorful northern and southern lights.

Remember those fireflies Scooby and Shaggy chased? They are another natural source of light. They have built-in flashlights because of bioluminescence.

How does it work? A special chemical reaction happens inside their bodies that makes them light up. This light doesn't produce heat. Instead, it's called cold light—and fireflies use it to "talk" to their friends!

FACT

Some jellyfish, deep-sea fish, and mushrooms use bioluminescence too!

Light made by something humans created comes from an artificial source. But don't let a label fake you out. Can you think of one of the most common sources of artificial light?

That's right! It's light bulbs. There are incandescent, fluorescent, and light-emitting diode (LED) bulbs. And even though they all work a little differently, they all use electricity to power them.

But light bulbs aren't the only source of artificial light. Other sources include candles, lasers, gas lamps, and fireworks.

Light Travels

Hang on, gang! There's still a whole lot more to learn about light.

Did you know that light travels in straight lines? Well, it does! Not only that, light travels through space at a whopping speed of 186,282 miles (299,793 kilometers) per second! That means it travels the 93.2 million miles (150 million km) from the sun to Earth in just 8 minutes and 20 seconds!

In one Earth year, light travels 5.88 trillion miles, or 9.46 trillion km, through space. We call that distance a light-year.

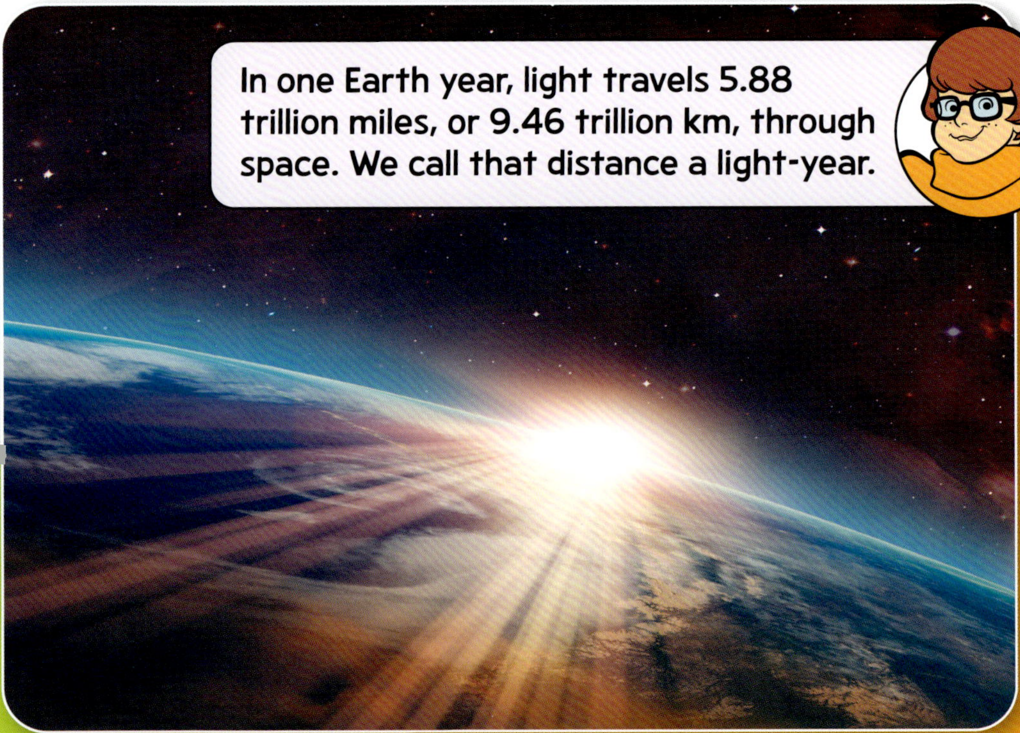

Light can travel fast, but can it pass through objects? It can through some things and can't through others.

If all the light can pass through an object, we say the object is transparent. Clear glass, like we have in many of our windows, is transparent.

When an object only lets some light through, we say it's translucent. Frosted glass, wax paper, and sunglasses are all translucent objects.

But some objects block light altogether. These are opaque objects. People are opaque. Things made of wood and metal are also opaque. When light hits these objects, it stops in its tracks. But something else happens too. Can you guess what?

Stand in the sunshine and look down. Do you see a dark shape of yourself on the ground? Your body has blocked the sunlight and cast a shadow.

Experiment with Shadow Puppets

WHAT YOU'LL NEED:

pencil
paper
scissors
tape
craft sticks
flashlight

WHAT TO DO:

1. Trace several animal or people shapes on the paper.
2. Use scissors to cut them out.
3. Tape each shape to the end of a craft stick to create simple puppets.
4. Turn off the lights and switch on the flashlight.
5. Place the puppets in front of the flashlight.
6. Move them around to see how their shadows dance and change on the wall.

Do you notice that the shadows are bigger when the puppets are closer to the flashlight? That's because the puppets are blocking more light when they are closer to the light source. The farther away you move the puppets, the less light they block. That's why their shadows get smaller.

Reflection and Refraction

Don't look now, but there are more mysteries to solve about light! Then again, looking might just be the thing to do! What we see depends on the way light behaves.

Look in a mirror. What do you see? You see yourself, of course! This is because light is reflecting off the mirror.

The reflection of light is kind of like bouncing a ball. When you throw a ball at a wall, it bounces right back at you. Light does that too. When light hits a smooth, shiny mirror, it bounces right back into your eyes and allows you to see yourself.

But light reflects off more than just mirrors. Everything we see reflects some light. Light bounces off objects and into our eyes. The furniture in your classroom reflects light. Playground equipment reflects light. Light even bounces off pets and other people, so we can see them.

But guess what happens when there is no light at all. That's right, we see nothing! That's because in total darkness, there is no light to reflect off the things around us.

Shaggy is having a problem with a broken straw. But is it really broken? What Shaggy doesn't know is that this is another special way light behaves.

Try it yourself. Stick a straw into a glass of water. Notice how the straw looks broken. Take it out of the water. Now it looks whole again! What is this trick?

It's not a trick. It's refraction. This means light bends when it passes through different transparent things. In other words, light travels faster through air, but it goes more slowly through water or glass.

Look closely at this example of a pencil in an empty glass versus in a glass of water. In the empty glass, light reflecting off the pencil must only pass through thin glass and air to reach your eyes. Because the light doesn't slow down and bend too much, the pencil still looks straight.

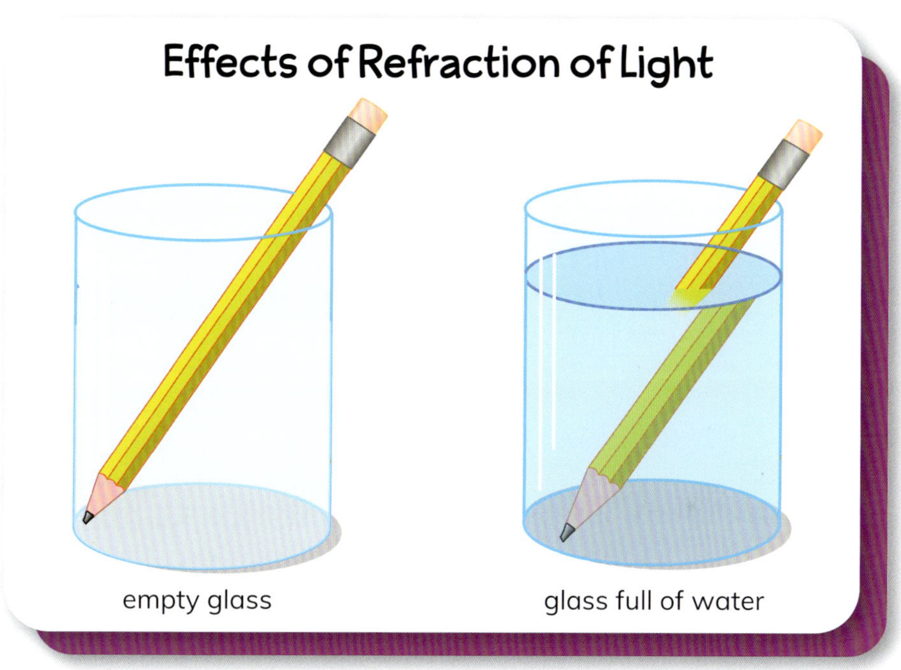

But light from the pencil under water has to pass through water, glass, and air before it reaches your eyes. The light changes speed while moving through each material. Because the light slows down and bends, the pencil looks broken.

FACT

Have you ever seen what looks like a puddle in a parking lot on a hot day? That's a mirage caused by light refracting through hot air.

The Rainbow Connection

Hey, gang! Do you remember that we said light is known as electromagnetic radiation? Well, it turns out many forms of radiation lie on the electromagnetic spectrum. All kinds of light are on that spectrum. This includes light we can see, or visible light, as well as light we can't see, or invisible light.

But wait! Why can we see some types of light and not others?

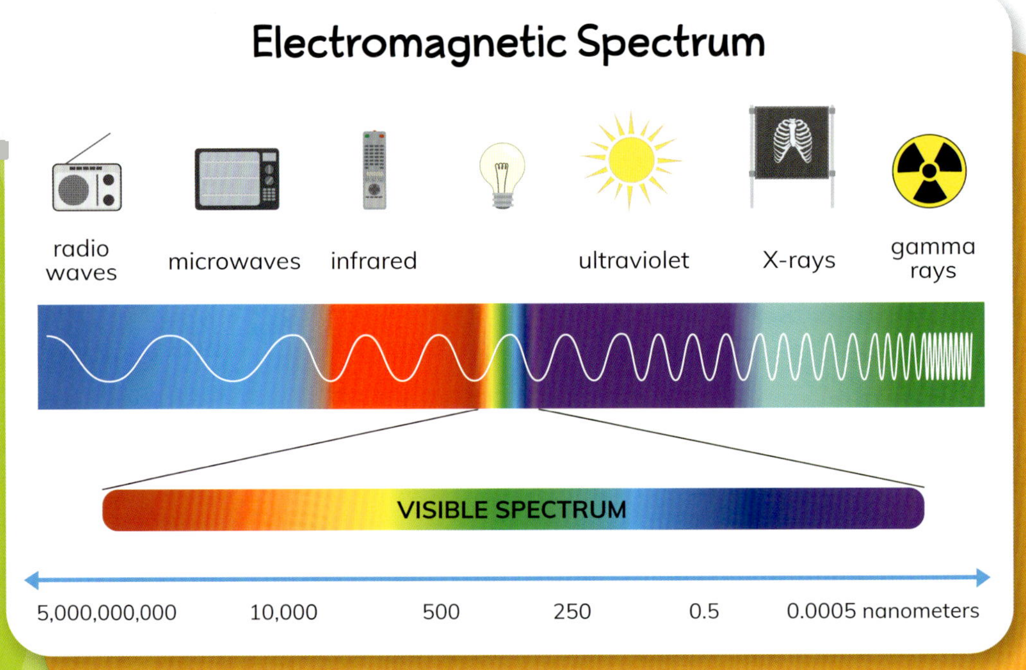

Light travels in waves. Just like ocean waves, some types of light have waves that are closer together. Others have waves that are farther apart. The distance between light's waves determines its wavelength. And our eyes can only see light waves of certain wavelengths.

On the electromagnetic spectrum, infrared light has a longer wavelength than visible light. Although we can't see infrared light, we can feel its heat. And we even use it. Night-vision goggles use infrared light to see in the dark. And remote controls use infrared light to turn on our TVs.

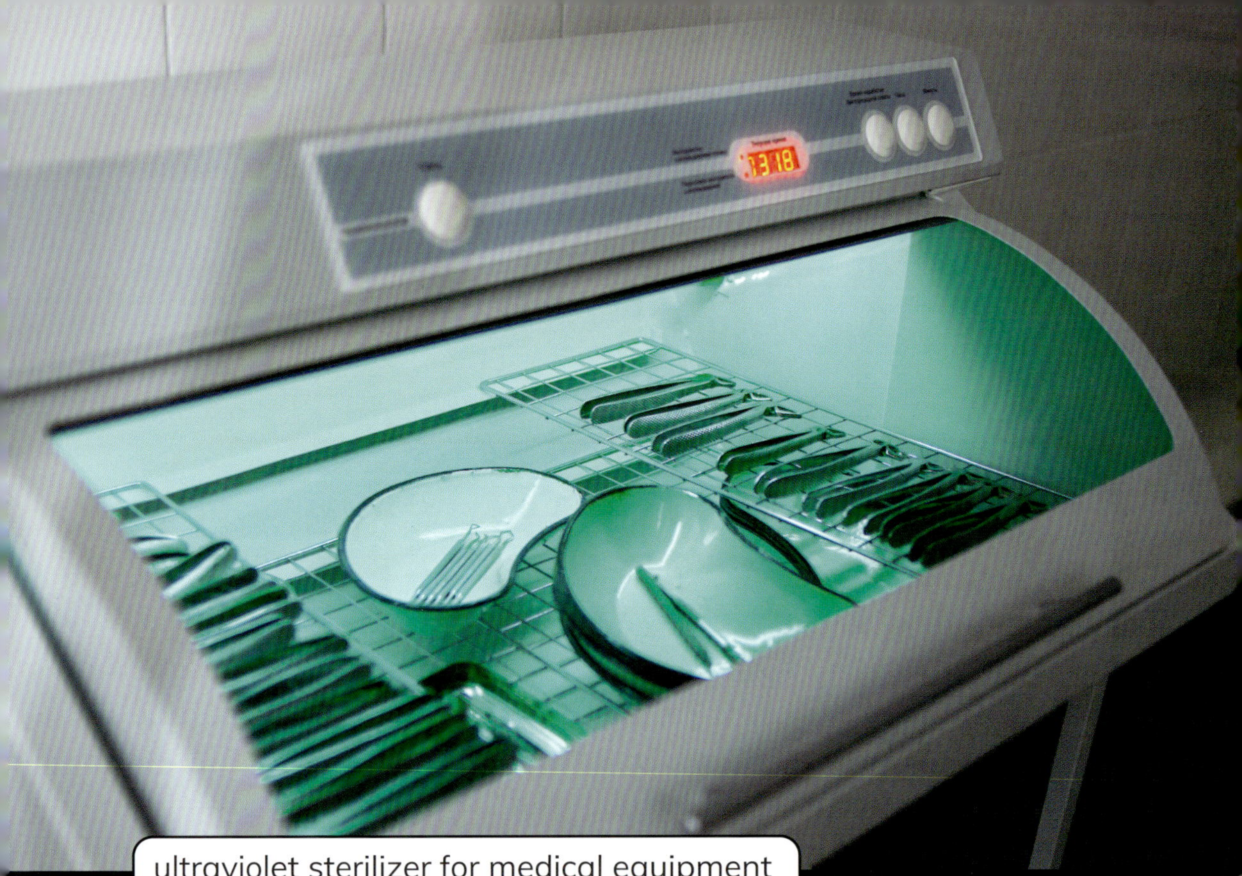

ultraviolet sterilizer for medical equipment

Near the other end of the electromagnetic spectrum is ultraviolet light. Its wavelength is shorter than visible light's wavelength. But just because we can't see it doesn't mean it isn't useful. Ultraviolet light is great for killing germs and bacteria, cleaning medical equipment, and purifying water. It's also used in bug zappers!

FACT

Scientists use ultraviolet light in the Hubble Space Telescope to get a fuller picture of what space is like beyond what our eyes can see.

In between ultraviolet and infrared light sits visible light. A long time ago, people thought visible light was white and rainbows were magic. But in 1666, a scientist named Sir Isaac Newton thought differently.

Newton suspected that a rainbow of colors was inside white light. To prove it, he performed an experiment using a triangular piece of glass, called a prism. When white light entered and exited the prism, the light bent and split into its rainbow of colors.

Sir Isaac Newton

prism

Wow, that's a cool rainbow!

That's refraction and reflection working as a team, just like us!

And that, gang, brings us to rainbows in the sky. They form when raindrops act like tiny prisms. As sunlight enters each raindrop, it refracts and then reflects off the back of the raindrop. When the light leaves the raindrop, it refracts again. This second refraction separates the light into the rainbow of colors we see in the sky.

FACT

Have you heard the acronym ROY-G-BIV? It's a way to remember the colors of the rainbow: red, orange, yellow, green, blue, indigo, and violet.

Make a Rainbow

WHAT YOU'LL NEED:

white sheet of paper

sunny window

water

clear drink glass

WHAT TO DO:

1. Place the sheet of paper on the floor or a table near a sunny window.
2. Fill the glass with water.
3. Place the glass on top of the paper.
4. See if you can spot a rainbow in the shadow the glass casts on paper.

The glass of water acts like a prism. The sunlight passing through it refracts and splits into the colors of the rainbow!

Eyes Like Cameras

So, gang, we've learned a lot about light so far. How it travels. How it bends. Even how it splits into a rainbow of colors. Now it's time to discover how our eyes use light to see the world around us.

The human eye is an amazing organ. When light reflects off objects, it enters the eye through a small hole called the pupil. Then it travels through a curved, jelly-like lens.

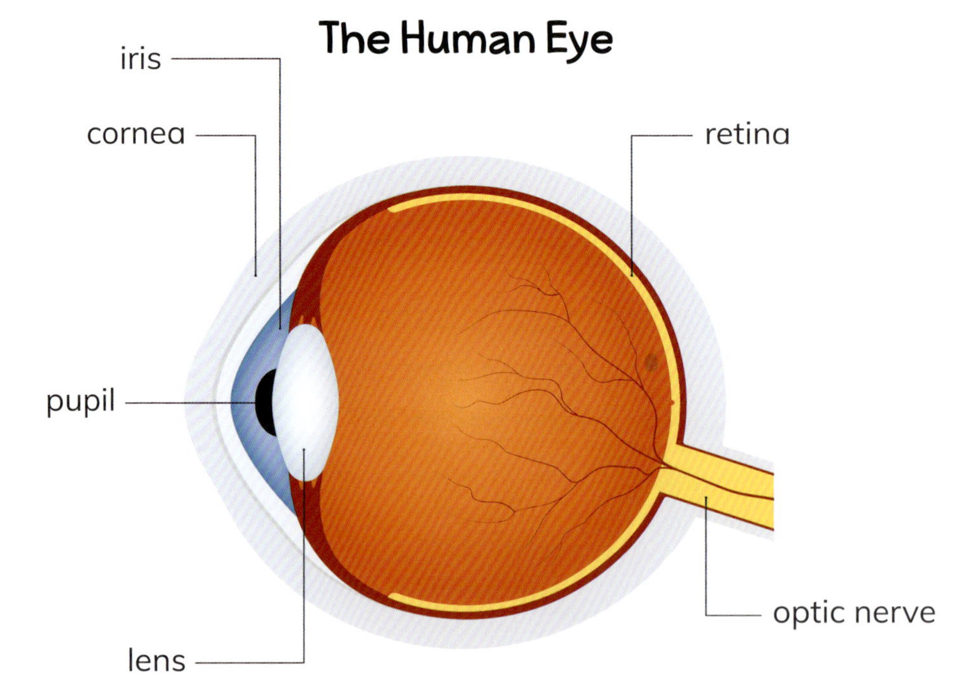

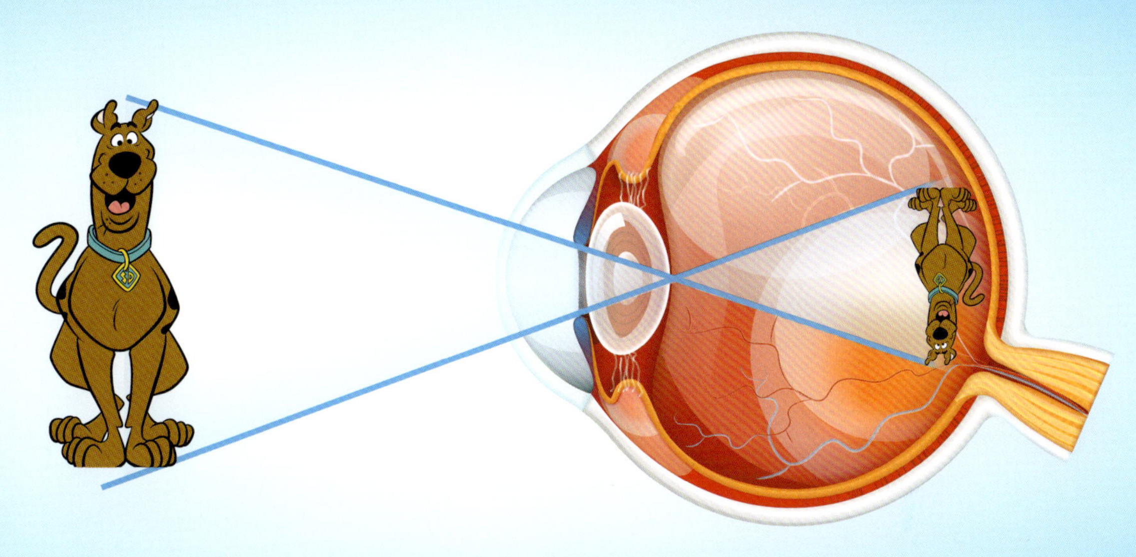

The lens focuses the light onto the retina at the back of the eye. But in the process, the lens also bends the light. Believe it or not, the bending light causes the image to appear upside down on the retina!

But fear not! The retina has special nerve cells. These cells send signals to the optic nerve which tells the brain what you're seeing. Then the brain turns the image right side up!

FACT

An old film camera works a lot like our eyes. It has an aperture similar to a pupil, a lens, and film much like a retina.

Make a Pinhole Camera

Without our brains, our eyes would see the world as upside down! To see what that would look like, try making a pinhole camera!

WHAT YOU'LL NEED:

scissors

shoe box

aluminum foil

masking tape

pushpin

wax paper

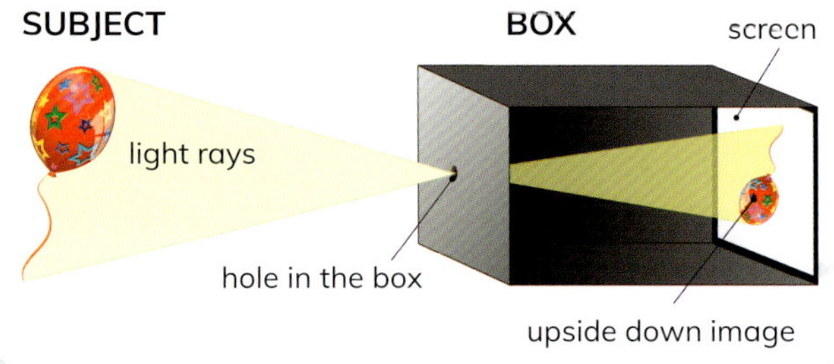

WHAT TO DO:

1. Cut a small square hole in one end of the shoe box.
2. Cut a piece of aluminum foil slightly larger than the hole you just made. Tape the foil over the hole.
3. Use a pushpin to poke a tiny hole in the center of the foil.
4. On the opposite end of the box, cut a larger square hole.
5. Tape a piece of wax paper over the square hole.
6. Make sure all other parts of the box are sealed with tape to prevent any light from entering except through the pinhole.
7. Point the pinhole toward a bright object outside. Look at the wax paper screen on the opposite end of the box.

What do you see? You should see an upside down image of the object outside.

FACT

Because light travels in straight lines, light beams cross as they enter the tiny pinhole. This is why the image is upside down on the screen.

Wow, gang! Light is super important for a whole bunch of reasons! It warms our planet and gives plants the ability to make food. It lets us see the colorful world around us and paints our skies with beautiful rainbows. It allows artists to take photographs and make movies. Light even helps scientists explore the universe!

Phew! Light sure does a lot. Now that you know a lot more about it, aren't you glad we have it?

GLOSSARY

acronym (AK-ruh-nim)—a word made from the first letters of the words in a phrase

aperture (AP-ur-chur)—a hole behind a camera lens that can be opened or closed to control the amount of light that shines onto the film

bioluminescence (buy-oh-loo-muh-NEH-senss)—the production of light by a living organism

electromagnetic radiation (i-lek-troh-mag-NET-ik ray-dee-AY-shuhn)—electromagnetic waves of all different lengths, including gamma rays, visible light, and radio waves, on the electromagnetic spectrum

infrared (IN-fruh-red)—light waves between visible light and microwaves on the electromagnetic spectrum

opaque (oh-PAKE)—blocking light

prism (PRIZ-uhm)—a transparent, triangle-shaped plastic or glass object that bends light

reflection (ree-FLEK-shuhn)—the change in direction of light bouncing off a surface

refraction (ri-FRAK-shun)—the bending of light; light is refracted when it travels through a prism or a lens

transparent (transs-PAIR-uhnt)—letting light through

ultraviolet (uhl-truh-VYE-uh-lit)—light waves between visible light and X-rays on the electromagnetic spectrum

READ MORE

Collins, Ailynn. *Exploring Light in Max Axiom's Lab.* North Mankato, MN: Capstone Press, 2025.

Gardner, Jane P. *Light and Sound.* Minneapolis: Bearport Publishing Company, 2023.

Musgrave, Ruth A. *All About Light.* New York: DK Publishing, 2023.

INTERNET SITES

Britannica Kids: Light
kids.britannica.com/kids/article/light/353386

Ducksters: Physics for Kids—Science of Light
ducksters.com/science/light.php

National Geographic Kids: Light and Lenses—10 Facts
natgeokids.com/uk/discover/science/general-science/light-and-lenses-10-facts

INDEX

ABOUT THE AUTHOR

Ailynn Collins has written many books for children, from stories about aliens and monsters, to books about science, space, and the future. These are her favorite subjects. She lives outside Seattle with her family and five dogs. When she's not writing, she enjoys participating in dog shows and dog sports.